FRASER VALLEY REGIONAL LIBRARY

39083507698364

D0116941

DISASTERS
PEOPLE IN PERIL

# DEADLY WAVES
## TSUNAMIS

TSUNAMI HAZARD ZONE

IN CASE OF EARTHQUAKE, GO
TO HIGH GROUND OR INLAND

**Mary Dodson Wade**

**Enslow Publishers, Inc.**
40 Industrial Road
Box 398
Berkeley Heights, NJ 07922
USA
http://www.enslow.com

Copyright © 2013 by Enslow Publishers, Inc.

All rights reserved.

No part of this book may be reproduced by any means
without the written permission of the publisher.

Original edition published as *Tsunami: Monster Waves* in 2002.

**Library of Congress Cataloging-in-Publication Data**

Wade, Mary Dodson.
  Deadly waves : tsunamis / Mary Dodson Wade.
    p. cm. — (Disasters—people in peril)
  "Original edition published as Tsunami: Monster Waves in 2002."
  Includes bibliographical references and index.
  Summary: "Examines tsunamis, including how they form and where they occur, what scientists can do to predict them,
and stories from survivors and witnesses to tsunamis around the world"—Provided by publisher.
  ISBN 978-0-7660-4018-2
  1. Tsunamis—Hawaii—History—20th century—Juvenile literature. 2. Tsunamis—Juvenile literature. I. Title.
  GC220.3.W34 2013
  551.47—dc22
                          2011044334
Future editions:
Paperback ISBN 978-1-4644-0109-1
ePUB ISBN 978-1-4645-1016-8
PDF ISBN 978-1-4646-1016-5

Printed in the United States of America

032012 Lake Book Manufacturing, Inc., Melrose Park, IL

10 9 8 7 6 5 4 3 2 1

**To Our Readers:** We have done our best to make sure all Internet addresses in this book were active and appropriate when we went to press. However, the author and the publisher have no control over and assume no liability for the material available on those Internet sites or on other Web sites they may link to. Any comments or suggestions can be sent by e-mail to comments@enslow.com or to the address on the back cover.

♻ Enslow Publishers, Inc., is committed to printing our books on recycled paper. The paper in every book contains 10% to 30% post-consumer waste (PCW). The cover board on the outside of each book contains 100% PCW. Our goal is to do our part to help young people and the environment too!

**Illustration Credits:** AP Images, p. 6; AP Images / Chris Stewart, p. 23; AP Images / David Guttenfelder, p. 41; AP Images / Dita Alangkara, p. 35; AP Images / Elizabeth Dalziel, p. 37; AP Images / Gemunu Amarasinghe, p. 18; AP Images / Harbor Branch Oceanographic Institution and NOAA, p. 31; AP Images / Kyodo News, pp. 4, 40; AP Images / Rick Rycroft, p. 11; AP Images / Sinopix / Rex Features, p. 42; AP Images / Wally Santana, p. 9; AP Images / Yasushi Kanno, The Yomiuri Shimbun, p. 26; AP Images / The Yomiuri Shimbun, p. 14; International Tsunami Information Centre / NOAA, p. 21; Pacific Tsunami Warning Center (PTWC), p. 29; Shutterstock.com, p. 1; Spencer Sutton / Photo Researchers, Inc., p. 12.

**Cover Illustration:** AP Images / Tomohiko Kano / Mainichi Shimbun / dapd (Tsunami wave in Japan, March 2011).

# CONTENTS

On April 1, 1946, as a tsunami struck the Hawaiian shores, Dr. Francis Shepard watched a "monstrous wall of water" sweep toward him. On March 11, 2011, the citizens of Japan witnessed the same disaster. In this photo, tsunami waves engulf the shores of Iwanuma in northern Japan.

# CHAPTER ONE

# "A MONSTROUS WALL OF WATER"

**WATER.** That's what everyone in Hawaii remembered about the morning of April 1, 1946. Dr. Francis Shepard, a marine geologist, had come to the island chain to study the effects of atomic bomb tests on a remote Pacific island. He and his wife stayed in a cottage on Oahu's north shore. They awakened to the sound of a dozen freight trains. Then a wall of water smashed through the front of their cottage, carrying the refrigerator, still upright, out the back door to a cane field.

The Shepards fled. They were shocked to see that there was almost nothing left of a nearby house. They raced to safety to a road on higher ground just as water overwhelmed their cottage. Then a "monstrous wall of water" swept toward them, "flattening the cane field with a terrifying sound."[1]

Eyewitness survivors on the "Big Island" of Hawaii, like sixteen-year-old Yasu Gusukuma, saw houses swirling in a "boiling" sea. Masao Uchima saw a fifteen-foot wave roll in. "I thought the whole island was sinking."[2] Behind it came a wall of water that stretched across Hilo bay.

This photo shows two views as a tremendous wave overwhelms Pier 1 at Kuhio wharf in Hilo, Hawaii, on April 1, 1946. An arrow points to a man caught in the torrent of water, one of the tsunami's 158 victims. The devastating waves reached a height of fifty-five feet on the coast of the Big Island.

Kapua Heuer's house sat on a sea cliff thirty feet above the harbor in Hilo on the Big Island. That morning, her daughter called out, "Mommy, why is there no water in the ocean?" From the edge of their cliff, they could see the water disappearing. Then a "great black wall" came back. With a roar, the water slammed into buildings, the lighthouse, and the railroad bridge. "Oh, that's good-bye to Hilo," Heuer said.

Paul Tallett noticed the strange dark-green color of the water. He saw the water recede, tumbling like big boulders as it went. He fled home yelling, "A big sea is coming!" And it did—a moving wall of water that came directly on shore.

The "big sea" arrived without warning. It reached a height of fifty-five feet on the northeast coast of the Big Island. But other islands felt its force as well. Molokai had fifty-three-foot waves, and waves on Kauai reached forty-five feet.[3]

The disaster happened on April 1, but it was no April Fools' joke. People lost their lives because the Hawaiian Islands are sitting ducks in the path of these tsunamis.

This was not the state's first tsunami, nor will it be the last. But it was Hawaii's worst—monster waves that brought death and destruction that day.

# CREATING A KILLER

**HAWAII IS A MAGICAL PLACE,** with picture-perfect sunsets, palm trees, sandy beaches, and surfers hanging ten on forty-foot curling waves. Visitors marvel at daily rainbows and brilliant tropical flowers. Even the island names are musical: Oahu, Maui, Kauai, Molokai, Lanai, and the Big Island of Hawaii. Many consider it paradise.

Why, then, did 158 people lose their lives there on that tragic April morning in 1946? The answer can be found in the ocean.

The Hawaiian Islands sit in the middle of the Pacific Ocean, formed by volcanoes. But violent spewing lava and volcanic dust did not cause deaths that day. Instead, massive waves took many lives.

Gigantic waves called tsunamis are the most powerful waves in the world.[1] The word *tsunami* is made up of two Japanese words. *Tsu* means "harbor," and *nami* means "wave."

Although the effects of a tsunami are seen most clearly in a harbor, they begin in the ocean. That's why some people call them tidal waves.

The devastated harbor of Soma in Fukushima prefecture, Japan, is filled with debris after the March 11, 2011, earthquake and tsunami. The effects of a tsunami are seen most clearly in a harbor, but the deadly waves begin deep in the ocean.

But tsunamis have nothing to do with ocean tides. Tides are caused by the gravitational pull of the moon and the sun. Most tsunamis are caused by water movement after an undersea earthquake.[2]

That has led some scientists to call them seismic sea waves. The word *seismic* refers to earthquakes, but that name is not exactly correct either. Other things besides undersea earthquakes can cause tsunamis.

A volcanic eruption near the ocean can also create a tsunami. The largest volcano-related tsunami happened when Krakatau (also called Krakatoa) in Indonesia erupted in 1883. Seawater rushed into the crater left by the explosion. This created a blast of steam so violent that it was heard as far away as Australia. The force caused a tsunami with waves several hundred feet high. It traveled around the earth, leaving a total of 36,417 people dead.[3]

On rare occasions, falling meteorites or huge rockslides can push aside enough water to cause a tsunami. A rockslide in Lituya Bay, Alaska, in 1958 caused a wave that left debris nearly a third of a mile up the face of the mountain across the bay. This run-up, the high point that the water reaches, is the highest ever recorded for a tsunami.[4]

Sometimes, underwater landslides are the source of a tsunami. Tons of rock shake loose and slide into deep trenches on the sea floor. When this is coupled with an earthquake, the tsunami gets even larger.

Normally, an undersea earthquake must measure 7.8 or larger on the Richter scale to cause a tsunami. However, in 1998, a medium-sized earthquake occurred off the coast of Papua New Guinea. Within five minutes, a thirty-five-foot wall of water came ashore. It killed more than

Villagers from Sissano, Papua New Guinea, search for salvageable material among the debris of several houses on July 21, 1998, after a tsunami struck the area. Although it typically requires a larger-scale earthquake to cause a tsunami, this magnitude-7 undersea quake created a tsunami that destroyed several villages on the island nation.

two thousand people. Why would a relatively small earthquake displace this much water? Scientists found evidence of a landslide into a deep ocean trench nearby.[5]

Most tsunamis occur in the Pacific Ocean. Japan has been keeping records of them for two thousand years. However, tsunamis have also been known to occur in the Atlantic Ocean and the Mediterranean Sea. They occur more often in the Pacific because 90 percent of the world's earthquakes occur around the Pacific Rim. The land bordering the Pacific Ocean has earned the name "Ring of Fire" for its volcanoes.[6]

Earthquakes occur when solid land masses called tectonic plates shift as they ride on molten rock deep in the earth. Plate edges grind against each other. Sometimes two plates get stuck. Even though the slipping stops, the force keeps building. When the plates break loose, the jolt causes an earthquake. Most of the time the plates move sideways without causing a tsunami.

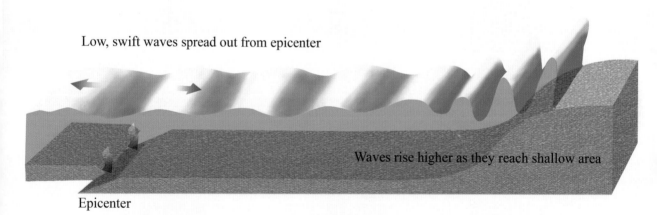

Low, swift waves spread out from epicenter

Waves rise higher as they reach shallow area

Epicenter

**This diagram shows the evolution of tsunami waves after an underwater earthquake.**

If, however, the edge of one plate rides up over the other, the second plate is forced down. Part of the ocean floor lifts, pushing the water above it upward. The other part of the ocean floor sinks, and the water over it drops down as well. Water rushes in to fill that space. This incredible movement of water creates a tsunami.

On April 1, 1946, there was a frightful displacement of water caused when an earthquake occurred off the coast of Alaska. Unimak Island, rising from the ocean some thirty miles from the deep Aleutian Trench, became the tsunami's first target.

At Scotch Cap, a desolate point on the island, a six-year-old lighthouse made of reinforced concrete sat forty feet above sea level. From its five-story tower, a powerful beacon blinked every fifteen seconds to guide ships along the coast. The lighthouse also had a foghorn to warn ships of the dangerous waters.

Five members of the Coast Guard lived at Scotch Cap and tended the light. Another sixty feet up the bluff above the lighthouse there was a radio direction-finding (DF) station. This was also maintained by a Coast Guard crew.

There wasn't much to do, and the crews often fought boredom by playing cards. On the evening of March 31, one of the DF crew came down to the lighthouse for a game of cards. A little after midnight, he left and walked up the hill to his sleeping quarters—just another night in this lonely place.

Then, at 1:30 A.M., a tremor shook the area for a minute, rattling the Coast Guard crewmen as items fell from shelves. The earthquake was large enough for instruments all over the world, including Hawaii, to record it. The operator at the DF station called down to the lighthouse. The crew below assured the radio operator that everything was okay. But nothing could have been further from the truth.

Twenty-seven minutes later, the earth heaved again as the edge of a tectonic plate snapped off and plunged into the Aleutian Trench. The sea floor dropped, an undersea landslide sent debris into the Aleutian Trench, and a gigantic tsunami rose out of the sea.

**Tsunamis move at remarkable speed and waves strike with tremendous power. In this photo, fishing boats are carried inland by ferocious waves during the March 2011 tsunami in Japan.**

Tsunamis move at incredible speed and strike with unbelievable power. Waves fan out just as ripples do on water when a rock is dropped into a pool. The area directly in front of the source of the wave will feel its main force, with lesser effect to the sides.

Oddly enough, the lifted water splits, sending one wave outward and one backward toward land, where it strikes quickly. Twenty minutes was all it took for the tsunami to strike Unimak. At 2:18 A.M., a wall of water smashed into the Scotch Cap lighthouse. Then it rode up the face of the cliff and flooded the engine room of the DF station. The crew there scrambled to higher ground.

From their high perch, the men strained to see the lighthouse beacon. They saw no light. There was no foghorn. The crew returned to the DF station and tried to contact the lighthouse by radio. There was no response.

As soon as it was light enough, the men walked to the edge of the cliff. An unbelievable sight greeted them. The lighthouse had vanished. The only thing left was part of the back wall of the building.

The DF station's radio operator sent out a message:

TIDAL WAVE PRECEDED BY EARTHQUAKE COMPLETELY DESTROYED SCOTCH CAP LIGHT STATION WITH LOSS OF ALL HANDS.... [7]

Scotch Cap lighthouse and its crew of five had been wiped off the face of the earth by a massive tsunami wave.

# NO PLACE
# TO HIDE

**WHILE ONE MASSIVE WAVE SWEPT AWAY** Scotch
Cap lighthouse, an identical wave raced through the darkness in the
direction of Hawaii. In the open ocean, tsunamis may reach maximum
speeds of almost 500 miles per hour, about as fast as a jumbo jet flies.[1]

Tsunamis come at Hawaii from all directions. Those from the
northwest begin off the coasts of Russia and Japan. Those from Peru
and Chile pound the islands from the southeast. But the worst ones
come from Alaska to the north. The killer tsunami that started in the
Aleutian Islands on April 1, 1946, arrived in paradise without warning.

It is almost impossible to detect a tsunami in the deep ocean. In mid-
ocean, the waves are usually no more than two to four feet high. Ships
pass over them without noticing.[2]

A fisherman in a boat off the coast of Hawaii felt nothing unusual
that morning. Looking outward to the sea, he observed a calm ocean.
Then he turned toward land and saw a huge wave crashing ashore.

The pilot of a small patrol plane saw something that looked like a line in the ocean. Unknown to him, it was the small rise of water caused by the tsunami. Curious, he radioed his base in Honolulu about what he had seen. His fellow servicemen just laughed. April Fools!

In spite of the jesting, the pilot was told to fly lower for a closer look. By that time, the line had disappeared. The wave had outrun his plane.

Less than five hours after the wave left Alaska, it struck Kauai's north coast just before 6:00 A.M. Seventeen people died.[3]

On the south side of the island, workers at the McBryde Sugar Company figured their supervisor was playing an April Fools' joke when he sent them to watch the tsunami from a cliff. They saw that the ocean had drained away. Fish were flopping in places where water had been. Then a huge wave came in, snapping trees as it went. Climbing down past fish tangled in tree branches, they scrambled back up as another wave appeared.

Tsunamis come in a series of waves. Even those people who know that more waves are coming may think they are safe when the first wave does not reach them. But the waves vary in size. Often the third to eighth waves are the largest.

The time between waves also varies. Some may be five minutes apart. With others, the time between one wave and the next may be as much as an hour and a half. Arrival times for waves depend on the distance between crests, or the top of the wave. Tsunami crests are much farther apart than the crests of waves caused by wind. Waves created by

**Waves crash through houses south of Colombo, Sri Lanka, on December 26, 2004, during a deadly tsunami. Tsunami waves can arrive at any part of the wave motion, but the most common way is as a flood of water.**

wind are rarely more than a thousand feet apart, about the length of two city blocks. Tsunami waves can be 60 to 120 miles apart.[4]

A tsunami may arrive at any part of the wave motion. Sometimes the trough, or low space in front of the crest, arrives first. When the trough comes in first, the water drains away from the land, leaving sea creatures stranded. When the crest and the trough arrive together, it creates a tumbling wall of churning water called a bore.

There is a popular notion that tsunamis are giant curling waves. A famous eighteenth-century painting by Japanese artist Hokusai shows a giant spilling wave towering over Mount Fuji. This shape is really a wind wave, but the painting represents the way most people think of tsunami waves. The most common way that a tsunami arrives is as a flood of water. It just keeps coming farther and farther inland.

Regardless of what form it takes, the water has tremendous force. It crushes whatever is in front of it. The force comes from the way the tsunami affects the water. Wind waves, even in large storms, disturb the water to a depth of no more than five hundred feet.[5] A tsunami wave is moving water all the way from the ocean floor to the surface.

As it speeds across the ocean, the wave loses little of its power. When the wave reaches land, it slows down. Millions of tons of water are moving. The slowing wave still has all the force behind it. Since the force can't move forward, the water piles higher. By the time they get to shore, the waves are enormous and deadly.

On that April day in 1946, the tsunami slowed as it struck Kauai. Then it moved to Maui and left fourteen people dead. By 6:30 A.M, it had claimed six more victims on Oahu.[6]

Heading for the Big Island, the tsunami seemed to have saved its deadliest fury for the last island in the chain.

# DISASTER ON THE BIG ISLAND

**SHORTLY BEFORE 7:00 A.M.,** the tsunami struck the Big Island, leaving more than one hundred people dead.

Wrapping around the island, it struck Hilo, on the eastern shore. The funnel-shaped harbor brought in the tsunami with incredible force. Businesses on Kamehameha Avenue, the main street of Hilo, were smashed. The train station disappeared. Railroad cars were thrown into the harbor. Wharf warehouses splintered. Docks collapsed.

The USS *Brigham Victory* sat in Hilo harbor, carrying fifty tons of dynamite. The first wave broke the mooring lines that held the ship to the dock. The crew started the engines to leave port. Steward Wayne Rasmussen saw the first wave and grabbed his camera. One of his photographs shows a helpless dock worker facing the wave that would engulf him.

The *Brigham Victory* steered around reefs to get into the ocean. On the way out of the harbor, the ship's crew rescued a truck driver who had been unloading sugar when his truck was swept into the bay.

Another worker, Tuk Wah Lee, fled to the rafters of a warehouse when he saw the brown wall of water. The wave ripped away the front of the building and shoved a barge through the back wall. When the water receded, Lee climbed down. After missing a line thrown by the ship's crew, he jumped and swam to the ship through debris. A sloshing wave lifted him enough so that he could scramble on deck; then it flattened the building where he had been.

Hilo, on the eastern shore of the Big Island, was destroyed by the 1946 tsunami. The harbor, streets, and homes were smashed by deadly waves.

Albert Yasuhara parked his soft-drink truck where he thought he would be safe and went to look. He had heard that tsunamis came in three waves. After the second wave smashed buildings, the bay emptied. Yasuhara saw the third wave reach halfway up the coconut trees. He and others fled up the street, just ahead of the water.

Jim Herkes stopped his car on the highway bridge over the Wailuku River. He and his brother watched as a wave struck the nearby railroad bridge and broke off one of the spans. When the wave retreated, the span sailed out under their feet. The next violent wave brought it back up the river. The railroad span came to rest 750 feet upstream.[1]

Bob "Steamy" Chow was a policeman on duty that morning. He saw the railroad span washing under the highway bridge. His job was to keep people out of the danger area. As he drove near the waterfront warning people to get out of danger, water swirled underneath his car. He had the helpless feeling that he was being washed away, but he lived to tell about it.[2]

Ninety-six people were killed in Hilo. Hardest hit was the low-lying Japanese community. The bayfront business district looked like a war zone. Then the wave moved on to Anaehoomalu where it took one more victim.

The total damage to the state of Hawaii amounted to $26 million in 1946 currency.[3] But no amount of money could pay for the damage done at Laupahoehoe.

Up the coast highway, about thirty miles north of Hilo, sits the community of Laupahoehoe. Its name comes from the lava rocks

Because of Hawaii's location in the Pacific Ocean, the island chain is susceptible to tsunamis from all directions. Although the April 1946 tsunami was deadly, Hawaiians have seen many more of the disasters. This photo shows a collapsed building from a tsunami wave following the massive earthquake in Japan on March 11, 2011.

(pahoehoe) that form the land. On that terrible day, the tsunami swept over the pahoehoe and claimed four people in the village below the cliff.

The school sat on a low point, with a seawall creating a level area for the baseball field. Teachers lived in cottages near the water. Fifteen schoolchildren and five teachers would lose their lives that day.

The school day had not yet started. Some children were out on the playground while others stood on the seawall looking at a curious sight.

The water had disappeared. The ocean floor was filled with all kinds of sea creatures flopping around. Some went down to pick them up.

Teacher Frank Kanzaki, eating breakfast at a friend's cottage, saw a giant wave rise out of the ocean. He grabbed the two little girls sitting at the table with him just as the wave struck and splintered the cottage. The water pulled one of the children out of his grasp. He never saw her again.

Third grader Carol Billena waited in her classroom. She thought the boy who ran past her was yelling "tiger wave." She asked her older sister if she could go out and see it. Her sister realized that he was saying "tidal wave." She pushed Carol out the door and pulled her up the hill. "Run, run, run!" she urged. Carol looked back. Cottages were breaking apart in the "boiling" sea. She could see heads bobbing in the water.

Martha Silva and her friend Janet De Caires had gone over to see turtles and fish washed up near the boys' bathroom. Janet wanted to go down to the water. "Stay with me," begged Martha. However, Janet ran to catch up with her brother and sister who were going to see the strange ocean sights. She got to the middle of the ball field before water as high as the coconut trees poured upon her and the other children in the low area. Martha fled up the hill. The next time she saw Janet's face, it was in a makeshift morgue.

Bunji Fujimoto thought it was an April Fools' joke when students said that the ocean had disappeared. His little brother went down to look, but Bunji hung back. He saw the wall of water rise over the seawall. Bunji's little brother was never found.[4]

# LEARNING FROM TRAGEDY

## TWO HOURS AFTER THE TSUNAMI HIT HAWAII,

the sea was calm again. By 9:00 A.M., boats were out picking up survivors. The grim task of identifying the victims began. Only 115 bodies were ever found.[1]

Laupahoehoe tenth grader Herbert Nishimoto was lucky. He was pulled out of the ocean the next day. Herbert was a strong swimmer who loved to dive into the rough water near his home at Laupahoehoe. Three-foot waves were nothing to him. He knew when to breathe during a dive. But this wave was different. It sucked him into the ocean.

Herbert kicked off his jeans in order to swim better, but one leg of his pants got caught on a reef. Dazed by the battering he received on the reef, he recovered enough to know that sharks and debris were all around. A bottle of cooking oil floated by. He had heard that swimmers greased their bodies, so he oiled himself. Part of a floor floated within his reach, and he heaved himself onto the boards.

About 1:00 P.M., a seaplane dropped a raft down to him and two other students. The three climbed in, but they had no paddle. After drifting all night, the exhausted boys were pulled ashore by two strong swimmers.[2]

For many years it was thought that 159 people died in the 1946 tsunami. Recently, researchers discovered that one of the schoolchildren,

**Just two hours after the tsunami hit Hawaii in 1946, the sea had calmed down. Although the tsunami may come and go quickly, the destruction it leaves behind lasts much longer. This is a view of Natori, Miyagi prefecture, Japan, after the earthquake and tsunami struck on March 11, 2011.**

an adopted child, had been counted twice—once with her Portuguese name and again with her Japanese name.[3]

Poet Juliet Kono wrote a poem called "School Boy From Up Mauka Way" to honor the children who died at Laupahoehoe. Into it, she wove the children's story called *The Five Chinese Brothers*. In the folktale, each brother saves another brother's life because he can do a special thing, such as swallowing the sea or stretching his legs. In Kono's poem, the water recedes as if swallowed by one Chinese brother. A child goes out to pick up red, gold, and silver fish, but the Chinese brother cannot hold the water. It returns, and the poet laments:

> *If I could, I'd have stretched my legs into stilts*
> *like the third Chinese brother*
> *and plucked you from the sea.*

But nobody was there to save the Laupahoehoe children from the churning flood of water.

Survivors of the disaster organized the Pacific Tsunami Museum to preserve their stories. The museum on Kamehameha Avenue stands in the area where the waves came ashore. Displays, photos, videos, and eyewitness accounts help visitors understand what happened. "Steamy" Chow's knowledge of the town provided accuracy for the model of Hilo prior to the 1946 tsunami.

Hawaii changed that day. Each April, during Tsunami Awareness Month, the museum sponsors a student essay contest. The city of Hilo built a park at the waterfront rather than replace buildings there. The park became larger after the 1960 tsunami crushed more buildings.

The old Laupahoehoe school yard is a park, too, with the school now high on the ridge. But no one forgets what happened out on that peninsula. Waves break on lava boulders near a monument honoring the students and teachers who died that day.

The tragedy brought worldwide action. The 1946 Hawaiian tsunami spurred scientists to find out more about this deadly phenomenon—why they occur and how the waves react. Still, it has taken time to learn about tsunamis because they are rare occurrences, and no two are alike.

The Pacific Tsunami Warning Center (PTWC) is one result of those efforts. PTWC is located on Oahu at Eva Beach not far from Pearl Harbor. As part of the National Oceanic and Atmospheric Administration (NOAA), it constantly records information about earthquakes and ocean water movement.

After 1960, when a Pacific-wide tsunami began in Chile, other countries formed the International Tsunami Warning System. This agency, under the direction of the United Nations, is also based in Honolulu. It coordinates efforts with the United States Tsunami Warning Centers, publishing information about tsunamis.

The PTWC issues alerts and warnings. Banks of satellite dishes gather information. E-mails, fax machines, and dedicated phone lines keep the staff in touch with other scientists all over the world. Someone is on duty at all times.

PTWC computers monitor hundreds of seismic stations around the world. Within minutes of an earthquake, they pinpoint the epicenter.

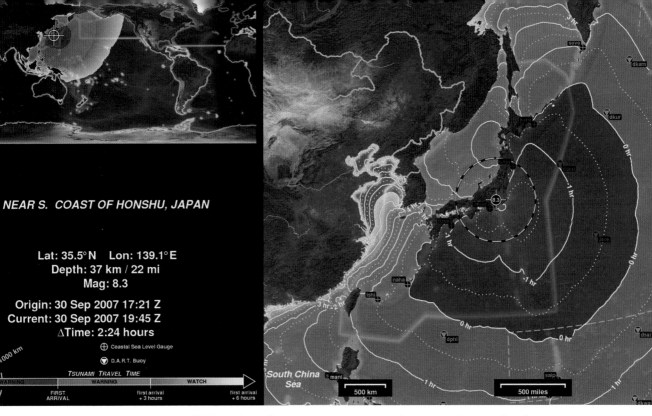

NEAR S. COAST OF HONSHU, JAPAN

Lat: 35.5° N   Lon: 139.1° E
Depth: 37 km / 22 mi
Mag: 8.3

Origin: 30 Sep 2007 17:21 Z
Current: 30 Sep 2007 19:45 Z
ΔTime: 2:24 hours

⊕ Coastal Sea Level Gauge
▽ D.A.R.T. Buoy

TSUNAMI TRAVEL TIME

| WARNING | WARNING | WATCH |
|---|---|---|
| FIRST ARRIVAL | first arrival +3 hours | first arrival +6 hours |

**The Pacific Tsunami Warning Center was created to monitor seismic activity and ocean water movement to help issue warnings and alerts to areas in danger. This map created by the PTWC shows the warning areas and approximate arrival times of the tsunami after an earthquake off the coast of Honshu, Japan.**

Recorders register data from a hundred tide stations outside Hawaii for signs of unusual surface water.[4]

For tsunamis, however, it is critical to know about water movement on the ocean floor. NOAA developed Deep-Ocean Assessment and Reporting of Tsunamis (DART®) to check for movement in deep water. The first six DARTs sat off the coast of Alaska and the northwestern United States. Following the huge Indian Ocean tsunami in 2004, more DARTs were added. There are now thirty-nine of them relaying vital information about Pacific Ocean conditions.

DART instruments, placed as deep as fifteen thousand feet, send signals to the surface. From there, the signal is relayed by satellite to PTWC every hour. However, when a tsunami wave passes by, DART reports it immediately. Second-generation DART IIs have been online since 2008. They not only report periodically, but they also can receive commands to send more frequent data when a tsunami is anticipated.[5]

When a large earthquake occurs, PTWC watches carefully for deep-water movement. If a large tsunami is detected, warnings go out to all areas along the path where a tsunami is possible. Radio and television announcements alert people with updates and advice.

The Hawaiian Islands, the most remote in the world, are so far away from other land areas that there is usually time to prepare. Scientists have learned that for every minute that a seismic (earthquake) wave takes to reach Hawaii, a tsunami will take one hour to arrive. In 1947, they developed a formal tsunami travel time chart.[6]

When a tsunami is confirmed, a warning plan goes into effect. Three hours before the tsunami is expected, Hawaiian Civil Defense sounds a three-minute steady siren. The siren sounds at hourly intervals and again a half hour before the wave is to arrive. People listen for announcements that update information.

This system works well for predicting distant tsunamis. But local tsunamis, such as the one that wiped out Scotch Cap lighthouse, occur within minutes. For that reason, the West Coast and Alaska Tsunami Warning System issue alerts for the northwest area of North America.

Workers aboard a ship prepare to drop a **DART** into the ocean. These deep-sea sensors, part of a tsunami warning system, send signals to the surface, which are then relayed to satellites. If a tsunami wave hits a **DART**, it is reported immediately.

Until recently, it was assumed that the mainland United States was safe from tsunamis. Actually, the 1946 tsunami brushed the California coast and killed one man. Then, in 1960, the Chilean tsunami sent waves all the way to Mendocino, California. The March 2011 tsunami that devastated Japan was also evident on the California coast.

Scientists are also concerned about tectonic plates grinding together off the coast of Washington and Oregon. The situation there is ripe for a tsunami-producing earthquake. In the 1980s, scientists found evidence that tsunamis had occurred in the region. An eleven-hundred-year-old layer of sand sits in Puget Sound in Washington State. Its arrangement matches the way that tsunami waves throw sand ashore.[7]

The Makah people were living in Washington long before it became a state. They have a legend about the sea draining away. When the water returned, it covered everything except the mountaintops. People who were carried away by the waves set up a new village off the coast of Vancouver Island in present-day British Columbia, Canada. The Makah legend is supported by the fact that people in the two places have very similar names. Also, Japanese records report a tsunami three hundred years ago in the same area that has telltale sand deposits of that age.[8]

Nothing can prevent a tsunami, but being informed can help people survive. The rules are simple: Seek high ground if there is a violent earthquake or if ocean water quickly drains away from land. Hawaii phone books give instructions and road signs to show safe evacuation routes. Ships and small boats should move to water six-hundred-feet deep or more.

Hawaii has learned hard lessons from the tsunamis it has experienced. More tsunamis will undoubtedly occur. But with a warning system in place, Hawaii won't have another tragedy like the one that happened on April 1, 1946. It will be ready, even if the tsunami turns out to have little effect, as during the 2011 Japanese event.

# CHAPTER SIX

# DISASTER IN THE INDIAN OCEAN

**A FEW MINUTES AFTER 3:00 P.M.** on Christmas Day 2004, the instruments at PTWC indicated that a large earthquake had occurred in the Indian Ocean. Across the International Date Line, at precisely 7:59 A.M. on December 26, 2004, a 750-mile long portion of the Burma tectonic plate had snapped off from the force of the Indian plate pushing against it. Plates that usually move only two and a half inches a year suddenly slipped fifty feet. The jolt of the movement resulted in a tsunami that claimed lives as far as 3,000 miles away.[1]

The earthquake epicenter was just off the northwest coast of the Indonesian island of Sumatra. The Indian Ocean had no tsunami warning system such as the PTWC provides. Death and destruction radiated out from the earthquake.

Staff at the PTWC alerted other observatories in the Pacific about the earthquake but underestimated its size. The magnitude was later fixed at 9.3 on the Richter scale. Ten minutes after the event, run-up waves as high as 113.4 feet washed over the northwest coast of Sumatra.[2] A fisherman from a village on the Sumatran coast felt the quake shake his boat. He saw water receding from the shore in classic tsunami style. Then with thundering noise, swirling water slung his boat toward land. He was later found clinging to a coconut tree two miles away from where his boat had been.

Tens of thousands of people were not so fortunate. Disaster swept westward to Africa and eastward to Thailand. At Banda Aceh on the northern tip of Sumatra, a nine-foot wall of water rushed inland for six miles across the flat landscape. Coastal fishing villages disappeared. Two hours later, Sri Lanka felt the blow. Within three and a half hours, the whole of the Maldives had been washed over. Eight hours later, three hundred people died on the east coast of Africa.

Waves traveling in the other direction struck the coast of Thailand, where many Europeans had come for the holidays. Videos and photos taken by vacationers caught images of tsunami waves crashing into resort areas.[3]

In the aftermath, people searched frantically for missing relatives. Bodies were brought to temples and preserved with dry ice. Families poured over photographs of the dead posted on walls. Mass graves were dug. In Sri Lanka, nine grieving mothers claimed a tiny baby boy who had been found on a beach among the bodies and debris. The baby boy was called "Baby 81" because he was the 81st admission to Kalmunai Hospital on the day he was found. A judge ordered DNA tests to determine the boy's real parents.

Residents walk through the remains of a market after massive waves struck Banda Aceh on Indonesia's Sumatra island. The water rushed inland for six miles across the flat landscape, destroying fishing villages.

Estimates of the dead and missing from all the affected countries on the rim of this disaster continued to rise. Six weeks after the event, the number had reached 280,000. Among them were at least thirty-three Americans known dead or presumed dead, with approximately eighteen missing. The exact numbers of casualties will never be known. Some of Indonesia's thousands of islands are remote—there is no one left to tell what happened. Remarkably, twenty-five days after the quake, the sole survivor of one island was rescued. He had lived by eating coconuts.[4]

The remoteness of some islands made it difficult to assess damage. Nicobar and Andaman islands north of Sumatra were hit hard. Hunter-gatherer tribes live on these two islands governed by India. They have little contact with outsiders. When Indian pilots flew over Andaman to look for survivors, inhabitants shot arrows at the helicopter. From all appearances, these people escaped harm. Scientists believe that the traditions of these people, whose ancestors came out of Africa 30,000 to 60,000 years ago, taught them to seek higher ground when earthquakes occur. Wild animals seem to have survived by a similar instinct.[5]

As pictures and reports streamed in, the world responded with money, equipment, and medical supplies. Health organizations feared epidemics of cholera and typhoid from lack of clean water. The USS *Lexington* aircraft carrier, with capability for making fresh water, steamed to Sumatra and stayed until adequate water was available. No widespread illness occurred, possibly because people did not crowd into refugee camps.

Roads, communication networks, businesses, houses, schools, and hospitals needed to be rebuilt. Japan promised $500 million in aid. The United States set government aid at $350 million. Former Presidents George H.W. Bush and Bill Clinton headed a campaign to encourage private donations. Celebrities raised money at benefit concerts.

The land takes time to heal—for rain to leach salt from rice fields so that crops will grow again. Fish and shrimp farms have to be rebuilt and stocked. Small farmers need livestock replaced. To coordinate this rebuilding process, the secretary-general of the United Nations

**Residents of Galle, Sri Lanka, walk through floodwaters in their town after it was hit by a tsunami in December 2004. Millions of people in the affected areas were in desperate need of aid—including food, clean water, and medicine—after the deadly disaster.**

appointed President Clinton as special tsunami envoy to accomplish the United Nation's goals.

Even amid all the devastation, however, there were moments of joy. DNA testing, funded by UNICEF (United Nations International Children's Emergency Fund), confirmed that Baby 81 was four-month-old Abilass Jeyarajah, son of Murugupillai and Jenita Jeyarajah. (The baby's name was taken from the Sanskrit word *abhilasha*, which means "desire" or "aspiration.")

After the court hearing, the Jeyarajahs took Abilass to a Hindu temple, where they gave thanks for his safe return. They also stopped to visit the remains of their former home, where the raging water had torn Abilass from his mother's arms. "Look how happy he is!" Murugupillai later proclaimed of his son. "After returning to us, he still hasn't cried."

According to the estimates of the United Nations, about 12,000 of the 31,000 lives lost to the tsunami in Sri Lanka were children. Approximately 1,000 children were left orphaned and more than 3,000 others lost one parent.[6]

Scientists noted effects that the earthquake and tsunami had left on our planet. Several islands moved slightly, including the island of Sumatra. This huge island, 1,060 miles long and 250 miles wide, shifted "a little over a meter, perhaps a couple of meters." The quake also wobbled the earth on its axis, altering the rotation of the planet so that the length of the day was reduced by 2.68 millionths of a second.[7]

The tragic loss of life and property in the tsunami led to more American DARTs being installed. Countries along the Pacific Ring of Fire developed a system to alert them to future Indian Ocean tsunamis. Sharing information between nations is vital. As Dr. Charles McCreery at the PTWC pointed out, "It's data coming from neighboring countries that's going to save you."[8]

# DOUBLE TRAGEDY IN JAPAN

## JAPAN HAS A LONG HISTORY OF EARTHQUAKES.

However, the one measuring 9.0 on the Richter scale that occurred on March 11, 2011, caused devastation not previously encountered. The earthquake occurred at 2:46 P.M. It was located thirty miles off the coast near the city of Sendai about 240 miles northeast of Tokyo. It had the double effect of crushing buildings and starting fires. Then a deadly twenty-three-foot tsunami surged inland for several miles.

The tsunami swallowed buildings and pushed anything that moved ahead of it—large fishing boats, cars, houses, splintered debris. Vehicles bobbed and ships at anchor smashed into each other. Remarkably, houses set on fire by broken gas lines burned amid all the water.

The flood of muddy water spilled over embankments and inundated farmland. It washed away roads, railroad tracks, and telephone lines. When the water retreated, the debris rode back with it. A tangled mess of trucks, cars, and buses lying on runways at the Sendai airport halted operations.

In this composite photo taken from a helicopter, the top frame shows a giant wave crashing into a residential area in Natori, Miyagi prefecture, Japan, during the tsunami on March 11, 2011. The bottom frame shows the same area about three months after the disaster. Only one house remains.

**A Japanese man walks through a flooded street in the ravaged city of Kesennuma, Japan, on March 27, 2011. The tsunami tossed debris everywhere, destroying fishing boats, harbors, farms, buildings, streets, railroad tracks, telephone lines, and anything else in its path.**

Unpredictable as always, the tsunami spread over the Pacific. The PTWC sent rapid alerts, but, unlike the Indian Ocean event, the Japanese event generated only small waves in Hawaii and other areas of the Pacific.[1]

For Japan, however, it was a different story. An estimated 15,700 people died, and thousands more were still missing.[2]

In addition to the loss of life, fishermen and farmers suffered loss of income. Fishing boats were smashed or swept out to sea, but an even more ominous problem loomed for them.

Farmers were affected, too. Their crops were ruined, and the fields need years to recover from the salt left by seawater. This time, however, both farmers and fishermen were confronted with a more dangerous problem—radiation from a disabled nuclear power plant.

Japan depends heavily on nuclear power. It had fifty-four nuclear plants on line when the tsunami occurred. At the Fukushima Daiichi

**Survivors take refuge at the Azuma Sports Park shelter about forty miles from the Fukushima Daiichi Nuclear Power Plant. The nuclear plant suffered serious damage during the earthquake and tsunami on March 11, 2011. The Japanese government relocated thousands of people to get them away from dangerous radiation leaking into the atmosphere.**

Nuclear Power Plant, water surged over the dike around the plant and knocked out the electrical system for cooling the radioactive rods.

Officials tried various methods of preventing the rods from melting. Attempts at using seawater were unsuccessful. Then contaminated cooling water had to be dealt with. Workers at the plant dumped the contaminated water into the ocean for a while. However, this was halted when people became afraid that it was contaminating the fish, a staple of their diet.

Several of the nuclear reactors suffered meltdowns or partial meltdowns as they overheated. Radiation was released into the air. More than one hundred thousand people living within twelve miles of the Daiichi plant had to leave. Some have returned, however, the worst contaminated areas around the plant will be uninhabitable for decades.

Fears of contaminated rice caused the Japanese government to set new radiation measurement standards for rice and for the soil it grows in.[3] Because of the devastation caused by the nuclear accident, the Japanese government mandated new safety measures for its nuclear power plants.

In spite of all the efforts to deal with the problems caused by earthquakes and the resulting tsunamis, these powerful forces of nature cannot be controlled. They cannot even be predicted with accuracy. However, with safety standards in place, a public educated to deal with tsunamis, and adequate warnings available, it is possible to avert huge loss of life. These are hard lessons learned from Lapahoehoe, Banda Aceh, and the Fukushima Daiichi Nuclear Power Plant.

# CHAPTER NOTES

## CHAPTER 1. "A MONSTROUS WALL OF WATER"

1. Francis P. Shepard, *The Earth Beneath the Sea* (Baltimore, Md.: Johns Hopkins University Press, 1959), p. 16.
2. Survivor stories recorded in Walter C. Dudley and Min Lee's *Tsunami!, in Tsunamis Remembered; Oral Histories of Survivors and Observers in Hawaii* (University of Hawaii), and video transcripts in the Pacific Tsunami Museum.
3. Karl V. Steinbrugge, *Earthquakes, Volcanoes, and Tsunamis: An Anatomy of Hazards* (New York: Kaskandia America Group, 1982), p. 246.

## CHAPTER 2. CREATING A KILLER

1. Frank I. González, "Tsunami!" *Scientific American*, May 1999, p. 58.
2. Ibid.
3. George Pararas-Carayannis, "The Great Tsunami of August 26, 1883 from the Explosion of the Krakatau Volcano ('Krakatoa') in Indonesia," n.d., <http://www.geocities.com/CapeCanaveral/Lab/1029/Tsunami1883Krakatoa.html> (April 3, 2001).
4. Anne M. Rosenthal, "The Next Wave," *California Wild*, spring 1999, <http://www.calacademy.org/calwild/archives/spring99/tsunamis.htm> (August 30, 2000).
5. R. Monastersky, "Seabed Slide Blamed for Deadly Tsunami," n.d., <http://www.sciencenews.org/sn_arc99/8_14_99/fob2.htm> (August 30, 2000).
6. Beth Rowen and Catherine McNiff, "Tsunami in Japan 2011," *Infoplease.com*, 2012, <http://www.infoplease.com/science/weather/japan-tsunami-2011.html> (January 18, 2012).
7. "Scotch Cap Lightstation Tsunami Disaster April 1, 1946," n.d., <http://www.teleport.com/~alany/uscg/ltsta.html> (April 3, 2001).

## CHAPTER 3. NO PLACE TO HIDE

1. *Tsunami*, n.d., <http://library.thinkquest.org/16132/html/tsunami.html> (April 3, 2001).
2. Frank I. González, "Tsunami!" *Scientific American*, May 1999 , p. 59.
3. Walter C. Dudley and Min Lee, *Tsunami!* 2d ed. (Honolulu: University of Hawaii Press, 1998), pp. 4, 41.
4. Ibid., pp. 118, 91; *Tsunami*.
5. Dudley and Lee, p. 90.
6. Ibid., pp. 4, 41–42.

## CHAPTER 4. DISASTER ON THE BIG ISLAND

1. Survivor stories recorded in Walter C. Dudley and Min Lee, *Tsunami!* 2d ed. (Honolulu: University of Hawaii Press, 1998), pp. 14, 15, 19–20, 17, 43.
2. Robert "Steamy" Chow, interview with author, Pacific Tsunami Museum, Hilo, Hawaii, March 6, 2001.
3. Frank I. González, "Tsunami!" *Scientific American*, May 1999, p. 64.
4. Lapahoehoe survivor stories found in Dudley and Lee, pp. 8, 10, 11, 42.

## CHAPTER 5. LEARNING FROM TRAGEDY

1. Walt Dudley and Scott C. S. Stone, *The Tsunami of 1946 and 1960 and the Devastation of Hilo Town* (Hilo: The Pacific Tsunami Museum, 2000), p. 16.
2. Herbert Nishimoto, video transcript, Pacific Tsunami Museum.
3. Donna Saiki, director, Pacific Tsunami Museum, e-mail to author, January 2, 2001.
4. Dr. Charles S. McCreery, interview with author, Pacific Tsunami Warning Center, Honolulu, Hawaii, March 5, 2001.
5. "Deep-ocean Assessment and Reporting of Tsunamis (DART®) Description," n.d., <http://www.ndbc.noaa.gov/dart/dart.shtml" (May 19, 2011).
6. Walter C. Dudley and Min Lee, *Tsunami!* 2d ed. (Honolulu: University of Hawaii Press, 1998), p. 102.
7. "Cascadia Earthquakes and Tsunami Hazard Studies," n.d., <http://walrus.wr.usgs.gov/cascadia> (August 30, 2000).
8. "Native American Legends of Tsunamis in the Pacific Northwest," n.d., <http://walrus.wr.usgs.gov/tsunami/NAlegends.html> (August 30, 2000).

## CHAPTER 6. DISASTER IN THE INDIAN OCEAN

1. "NOAA and the Indian Ocean Tsunami," n.d., <http://www.noaanews.noaa.gov/stories2004/S2358.htm> (February 3, 2005).
2. "The Distribution of the Tsunami Hights [sic] in Banda Aceh Measured by the Team Dr. Tsuji Leads," n.d., <http://www.eri.u-tokyo.ac.jp/namegaya/sumatera/surveylog/eindex.htm> (February 4, 2005).
3. Michael Elliott, "Sea of Sorrow," *Time*, January 10, 2005, pp. 30–33.
4. "Indonesia Toll From Tsunami Disaster Rises to 238,946," January 28, 2005, *ABC News*, <http://www.bloomberg.com/apps/news?pid=10000080&sid=a40T9tNz2tbM&refer=asia> (February 4, 2005).
5. "Did Island Tribes Use Ancient Lore to Evade Tsunami?" January 25, 2005, <http://news.nationalgeographic.com/news/2005/01/0125_050125_tsunami_island.html> (January 27, 2005).
6. Krishan Francis, "Tsunami Child 'Baby 81,' Parents Reunited," *Associated Press, Yahoo! News*, February 16, 2005, <http://news.yahoo.com/> (February 16, 2005).
7. Jim Loney, "Asia Quake, Tsunami Moved Islands, Shortened Days," *Reuters, Yahoo! News*, February 10, 2005, <http://news.yahoo.com/> (February 25, 2005).
8. Dr. Charles S. McCreery, telephone interview with author, February 4, 2005.

## CHAPTER 7. DOUBLE TRAGEDY IN JAPAN

1. "Japan Earthquake 2011: 8.9 Magnitude Earthquake Hits, 30-Foot Tsunami Triggered," *Huffington Post*, March 11, 2011, <http://www.huffingtonpost.com/2011/03/11/japan-earthquake-tsunami_n_834380.html> (May 26, 2011).
2. "Japan Tohoku tsunami and earthquake: The death toll is climbing again," *Earthquake-Report*, August 15, 2011, <earthquake-report.com/2011/08/04/japan-tsunami-following-up-the-aftermath-part-16-june/> (October 20, 2011).
3. Shino Yuasa "Japan Earthquake 2011: New Search For Bodies Launches," *Huffington Post*, April 9, 2011, <http://www.huffingtonpost.com/2011/04/10/japan-eartquake-2011-new-bodies-search_n_847115.html> (May 14, 2011).

# GLOSSARY

**bore**—Churning water that is moving over the top of water moving the opposite way.

**crest**—The top of a wave.

**debris**—Scattered pieces of an object that has been destroyed.

**distant tsunami**—Giant wave that occurs as the result of an earthquake far away.

**interval**—A set time between two actions.

**local tsunami**—Giant wave that occurs as the result of a nearby earthquake.

**mooring lines**—Chains or ropes used to tie a ship to a dock.

**pahoehoe**—Hawaiian name for lava that is the hardened shape of flowing molten rock.

**peninsula**—Land surrounded by water on three sides.

**radio direction-finding (DF) station**—A radio station that sends out signals to guide ships and airplanes.

**run-up wave**—The high point reached by a tsunami wave.

**seabed**—The ocean floor.

**seawall**—A stone or concrete wall that forms a barrier against the ocean.

**seismic**—Earth's vibration; something having to do with earthquakes.

**span**—A section of a bridge.

**supervisor**—The person in charge of a group of workers.

**tectonic plates**—Sections of the earth's crust that move over molten material deep below the surface.

**trough**—The empty space in front of the wave crest.

**tsunami warning**—An announcement that a tsunami is approaching.

**tsunami watch**—An announcement that a tsunami may occur.

**wind waves**—Waves caused by wind blowing on water.

# FURTHER READING

## BOOKS

Dwyer, Helen. *Tsunamis*. Tarrytown, N.Y.: Marshall Cavendish Benchmark, 2011.

Fradin, Judy, and Dennis Fradin. *Tsunamis*. Washington, D.C.: National Geographic Society, 2008.

Kusky, Timothy. *Tsunamis: Giant Waves From the Sea*. New York: Facts on File, 2008.

Walker, Niki. *Tsunami Alert!* New York: Crabtree Publishing Company, 2006.

Woods, Michael, and Mary B. Woods. *Tsunamis*. Minneapolis, Minn.: Lerner Publications, 2007.

## INTERNET ADDRESSES

National Oceanic and Atmospheric Administration (NOAA): Tsunami
<http://www.tsunami.noaa.gov/>

Pacific Tsunami Museum
<http://www.tsunami.org/>

Tsunami!: Tsunamis—Past and Present
<http://www.ess.washington.edu/tsunami/index.html>

# INDEX